SUMMARY & ANALYSIS

OF

FIGURING

A GUIDE TO THE BOOK
BY MARIA POPOVA

NOTE: This book is a summary and analysis and is meant as a companion to, not a replacement for, the original book.
Please follow this link to purchase a copy of the original book: **https://amzn.to/2XTCyHU**

Copyright © 2019 by ZIP Reads. All rights reserved. This book or parts thereof may not be reproduced in any form, stored in any retrieval system, or transmitted in any form by any means—electronic, mechanical, photocopy, recording, or otherwise—without prior written permission of the publisher, except as provided by United States of America copyright law. This book is intended as a companion to, not a replacement for the original book. ZIP Reads is wholly responsible for this content and is not associated with the original author in any way.

TABLE OF CONTENTS

SYNOPSIS 5

CHAPTER SUMMARIES & KEY TAKEAWAYS 7

JOHANNES KEPLER 7

MARIA MITCHELL 9

TRUTH & BEAUTY 11

MELVILLE & HAWTHORNE 12

MARY SOMERVILLE & ELIZABETH BARRETT BROWNING 13

LOVE & DEATH 15

MARGARET FULLER'S CONVERSATIONS 18

WALDO & MARGARET 19

FULLER'S REVOLUTION OF THOUGHT 20

WOMEN & EDUCATION 22

MARAGRET'S LOVE 23

LIFE IN ROME.. 24

ILLNESS.. 26

CAMERA OBSCURA 27

HARRIET HOSMER 29

LIFE, LOVE & LOSS 31

EMILY DICKINSON	32
PALE BLUE DOT	36
RACHEL CARSON	37
NUCLEAR FISSION	41
RACHEL CARSON'S LEGACY	42
INTO THE SEA	46
KEY THEMES	**47**
EDITORIAL REVIEW	**51**
TIMELINE OF EVENTS	**53**
BACKGROUND ON AUTHOR	**55**

SYNOPSIS

Figuring is Maria Popova's genre-bending analysis and reflection on the human condition through the works of some of the greatest scientists, authors, and thinkers throughout history. Beginning with Johannes Kepler's discovery of the laws of planetary motion and weaving delicately through centuries of discovery and social change, she ends with ecologist and author, Rachel Carson.

The book is divided into twenty-nine chapters that follow a mostly-chronological path from Kepler to Carson, however histories and timelines are frequently jumped between as she links together the lives of so many well-known characters throughout history. In addition to Kepler and Carson, Popova focuses on the lives of Maria Mitchell, Margaret Fuller, Harriet Hosmer, and Emily Dickinson, but it would be a disservice to limit a synopsis to those women. The timeline, mostly taking place in the nineteenth century, is strewn with familiar names like Emerson, Thoreau, Melville, Darwin, Hawthorne, Browning, and Whitman.

For each historical figure, scientist, or persona she mentions, their lives, childhoods, careers, families, and loves are intricately intertwined with their contemporaries, with their idols, and with those they would come to inspire, including Popova herself. The book is rich with excerpts from their poetry, their novels, and their personal letters. For the purpose of this summary, not every chapter is summarized individually, but rather organized by subject.

Beyond just the social, scientific, and literary contributions of those studied, the book takes a particular look at feminism and sexuality. Many of the women profiled were perhaps lesbians, though the word didn't exist yet in their time. Instead, she investigates the meaning of uncommon love, of bonds that defy the lexicon of any particular era, and allows each love letter overflowing with ardor and exultation to tell its own piece of the larger story of the woman or man who wrote it.

The overall journey is one from the beginnings of the Enlightenment to spiritual transcendentalism and feminism in the nineteenth century, finally leading to the environmentalist movement of the twentieth—each previous era and its most notable inhabitants informing the development of the collective conscious in the next. The ultimate thesis of the book is one of a vast interconnectedness that the transcendentalists and Rachel Carson knew so well: that there is no science without art and no art without science.

CHAPTER SUMMARIES & KEY TAKEAWAYS

JOHANNES KEPLER

"O the cares of man, how much of everything is futile" – Perseus

Key Takeaway: Johannes Kepler discovered elliptical orbits.

Though Copernicus's heliocentric model had been presented about fifty years prior, Kepler was the first to discover and measure the elliptical orbits of the planets. Galileo, who at the time also believed in the Copernican model, was too afraid to speak out for the consequences of such blasphemy. Kepler paid the price and was banished from the seminary and forbidden from speaking at the pulpit.

After his banishment, he headed to Prague at the invitation of Tycho Brahe, the royal mathematician to the Holy Roman Emperor. With Brahe's sudden death, Kepler was given the position along with access to all of Tycho's astronomical data, aiding greatly in his calculations of the orbits.

Key Takeaway: Kepler predicted the force of gravity where Copernicus failed.

Copernicus, while correct about the heliocentric model, still saw the movement of the planets as circular and believed it driven by a Godly force. Kepler believed there was something else at play, predicting the existence of gravity and gravitation pull at the Earth's surface long before Newtonian physics came into being. In fact, Newton took Kepler's three laws of planetary motion and refined them in his own work on laws of motion and universal gravitation.

Key Takeaway: In 1608 Johannes Kepler wrote his science-fiction manuscript, *Somnium*.

Somnium, Latin for *'The Dream'* was perhaps the first science-fiction book ever written. It predicted space travel 300 years before it was a reality. The story was of a society of people who live on the moon and believe that the Earth revolves around them and that the moon remains perfectly still. Each day they see the Earth rise and set as we on Earth see the Sun. The purpose was to present the ignorance of humanity—refusing to believe the Copernican, heliocentric model was equally as ridiculous as the believing the Earth revolved around the moon.

Unfortunately, the people weren't ready for his allegory and they took his story all too literally. A character in the book based on his mother was a witch, and the ignorant townspeople from his home town pounced on the opportunity. He spent six years fighting for his mother's freedom. Though he was able to save his mother, Kepler died before he could finish typesetting *The Dream*. It wouldn't be published until 1634 by his son.

MARIA MITCHELL

The second chapter opens with the story of a young Quaker girl looking through her telescope in Nantucket in 1831. Women cannot vote, they cannot receive an education in the sciences, and they will not be hired for any technical careers. But Maria Mitchell would become the world's first professional female astronomer, and the first female astronomy professor, eventually working for the Navy as a "computer of Venus," a prestigious position as a mathematical astronomer as well as director of the Vassar College Observatory.

Key Takeaway: Maria Mitchell discovers a new comet.

In a contest led by the Dutch King in 1847, anyone who could discover and chart the course of a new comet would be awarded with a valuable gold medal. At the age of 29, Mitchell won the prize. The next year she was the first woman elected to membership in the American Academy of Arts and Sciences.

Key Takeaway: We are both products of ourselves and products of our environment.

That Maria grew up on the island of Nantucket, where the mathematics of navigation were a common thing, in a Quaker family who valued the equal education of boys and girls surely played some part in who she turned out to be. But her natural proclivity for math and curiosity about the heavens—in a place where astronomy was one of the few things to do—also played their roles. This balance between nature and nurture is a theme that Popova return to throughout the book.

Key Takeaway: Caroline Herschel was a role model of Maria Mitchell's.

Herschel, who got into astronomy to help her brother and realized she was better at the calculations than he was, set out in 1782 to fix numerous errors she had found in John Flamsteed's famous star catalogue. Flamsteed's catalogue lacked an index and, in the process of correcting his errors, Herschel discovered a missing nebula and the dwarf elliptical galaxy called Messier 110. In her life, she calculated the locations of 2,510 nebulae and discovered eight comets. For this she was the first woman awarded with the Gold Medal from the Royal Astronomical Society. Another woman wouldn't receive it for 168 years.

TRUTH & BEAUTY

"Beauty is the form under which the intellect prefers to study the world" – Ralph Waldo Emerson

Key Takeaway: Maria Mitchell fought for social justice.

Beyond her work towards women's rights in the sciences, Mitchell was also a close friend of Frederick Douglass's and used her Nantucket Atheneum—a place of open intellectual discourse that she managed for twenty years—to promote abolitionist causes as well. Ralph Waldo Emerson was also a guest speaker, and Mitchell taught him how to use a telescope.

Key Takeaway: There is an undeniable connection between truth and beauty, between science and art, between astronomy and poetry.

Much of the chapter focuses on the intersection between science and art—that Emerson was so enamored with the beauty of the night sky and that Mitchell was so inspired by poetry. It wasn't until Galileo that Euclidian geometry and perspective were blended with the art of celestial drawings, suggesting the truth of the moon's rocky surface. Mitchell said in her diary that "Euclid alone has looked on Beauty bare" (Popova, p. 59), speaking to the raw beauty of his immutable geometric truth—free from human judgment or opinion.

Key Takeaway: Mitchell found a strange love with Ida Russell.

Though the true nature of their relationship remains speculation, the author believes that they were more than just friends and asserts that Russell was likely the love of Mitchell's life. The book also includes Mitchell's ruminations on the nature of love and friendship—that each person we love fulfills a different part of what we need so that in a circle of friends, all of those needs can be met.

MELVILLE & HAWTHORNE

Key Takeaway: Herman Melville and Nathaniel Hawthorne had an intense relationship.

Popova shares excerpts of letters and poems between the two very close friends which suggest that Melville was in love with Hawthorne, though it was potentially unrequited. Melville wrote long, amorous, and glowing reviews of Hawthorne's books and wrote letters that cannot be mistaken for anything but love letters. The two men lived just six miles apart from one another and surely had many evenings of brandy, cigars, and philosophical discussions. But ultimately, Melville's fervor proved too much for Hawthorne, and he withdrew from the relationship. Melville, even forty years later, would still write about that sting of rejection.

Key Takeaway: Human love defies definition.

Whether Maria and Ida or Herman and Nathaniel ever had physical relationships is beyond impossible to guess. Regardless, the author opines on the unnamable nature of love. At the time, choosing to go unmarried as a bachelor or spinster was a radical choice, and likely Melville, Russell, Mitchell, and Hawthorne were all pegged as "other" at one point in their lives. Perhaps their loves were platonic, perhaps more, but naming these relationships as "other" or "queer" defies the very nature of infinite human love.

MARY SOMERVILLE & ELIZABETH BARRETT BROWNING

Mary Somerville, a Scottish mathematician and author, was one of Maria Mitchell's few living heroes. She was also the math tutor of Lord Byron's only legitimate child, Ada Byron. Mitchell compared Somerville, Elizabeth Barrett Browning, and Caroline Herschel as examples of "few women of genius who have become the successful rivals of man in the paths which they have severally chosen." (Popova, p. 74). The chapter goes on to discuss the genius of Somerville and Barrett Browning's work in detail.

Key Takeaway: Somerville's *Connexion* was an unprecedented synthesis of scientific fields.

After writing a brilliant and expanding translation of a mathematic treatise of Pierre Simon-LaPlace, Somerville eventually released it as a standalone book, *The Mechanism of the Heavens* in 1831 and was met with wide critical success. *On the Connexion of the Physical Sciences*, released in 1834, was one of the bestselling scientific books of the nineteenth century. Twenty-five years later, Mitchell would celebrate it as a masterpiece. William Whewell, master of Trinity College, was instrumental in making the LaPlace translation a requirement of Trinity's curriculum, and he coined the term "scientist" for Somerville in place of "man of science."

Key Takeaway: Mitchell and Whewell butt heads.

By the time Maria Mitchell met Whewell twenty-five years later, she found a pretentious, pompous, and close-minded man whom she was unable to reconcile with his brilliant work. Whewell scoffed at Mitchell for her love of Elizabeth Barret Browning's epic novel, *Aurora Leigh* and openly criticized Emerson. Though a famous scientist herself, Mitchell held Barrett Browning and Emerson in much higher esteem than many of her scientific contemporaries.

Key Takeaway: *Aurora Leigh* leaves a lasting impression.

Popova goes into great detail on the plot of *Aurora Leigh*, the tale of a woman who becomes a poet, shuns the idea of marriage to a man who doesn't appreciate her art, and embraces her poverty and self-sufficiency. Romney, the man she was to marry, falls in love with a poor girl well below his station in life. Aurora can't object as the girl is honest and kind. On the day of the wedding however, the poor girl disappears after being convinced she isn't good enough for Romney. She is brutally gang-raped and impregnated. Aurora sees her on the street and vows to raise her child together, but the girl is already dead inside. She is incapable of loving anyone or anything.

Barrett Browning's vivid, brutal description of rape and her embracing of interclass marriage and female self-sufficiency were radical ideas. Most of all, however, she saw art as a transformative tool for truth, the human heart, and the world—art and life were one and could never be disentwined. *Aurora Leigh* would impact Mitchell more than any other work.

LOVE & DEATH

Centuries past have been rife with untimely death and disease, making a belief in an immortal soul that much more of a comfort when faced with so much tragedy. Scientists and philosophers, however, often find no comfort in such fantasies, seeing them too much for what they are. Popova takes a detailed look at the romantic ties and metaphysical beliefs of Margaret Fuller and Richard Feynman.

Key Takeaway: Nobel Prize-winning physicist Feynmen reaches for the afterlife.

In a letter discovered during research for a biography of the famous physicist in 1988, Feynman writes to his wife, Arline, who had died two years prior of tuberculosis. Despite him being fervently rooted in science, reason, and medicine, he longed for the comfort of the afterlife in her passing despite believing it was unreal, a sentiment that Barrett Browning had echoed in *Aurora Leigh*.

Key Takeaway: Margaret Fuller informed her beliefs on love through Goethe.

Fuller, who wrote the seminal work *Women in the Nineteenth Century*, and who was the inspiration for *Aurora Leigh*, could not reconcile her intellect with the dogmatic religious beliefs of her time. She was a singular and determined mind whose father gave her every educational opportunity a young boy would have had, likely because he wished she was one. She was extremely well-read, spoke several languages, and fell in love with the writings of Goethe after teaching herself German. His concept of "the All"—living beyond yourself and expanding into all of existence—spoke to her in the same way it spoke to Emerson, whom she eventually had an intimate, yet often confusing, relationship with.

Key Takeaway: Science informed the poetry of the time.

When Melville wrote Hawthorne and when Fuller wrote a series of sonnets for a woman she loved named Anna Barker, they both spoke of a "divine magnet" pulling them towards the objects of their affections. The author contends that magnetism was an exciting scientific discovery of the time and Fuller's muse, Goethe, was "the supreme cross-pollinator of nineteenth-century science and poetry" (Popova, p. 112).

Key Takeaway: Transcendentalism defined the philosophical current sweeping through New England at the time.

More and more, artists and intellectuals were looking inwards to experience spirituality and believing that social reform was driven first by personal reform—that all things came from within. This was in hard opposition to the strict and dogmatic religious teachings of the time.

"What lies behind us, and what lies before us are tiny matters compared to what lies within us." – Ralph Waldo Emerson

MARGARET FULLER'S CONVERSATIONS

Key Takeaway: Fuller pioneered education as conversation over lecture.

At the time, teaching was the only option available for single women to support themselves. Most however, would quit as soon as they married. Fuller and her close friend Elizabeth Peabody were devoted to inspiring young women to break out of the meek listeners they were trained to be—to embrace independent thought and stimulating conversation and to transcend the banal through the lens of beauty.

Outside of school, in 1839, Fuller started a series of meetings called "Conversations" held at Peabody's home where women would come together, encouraged to discourse, critical thinking, creativity, and independence of thought. Where many other intellectual meetings at the time were forbidden for women, and were presented in a one-to-many lecture format, these Conversations were wholly different. The series even inspired a groundbreaking magazine collaboration with Emerson, known as *The Dial*—the first fully independent publication unbeholden to the church or institutional academia based on the tenets of transcendentalism.

Key Takeaway: Fuller demanded "the All" from her romantic partners.

Time and again, the intensity of Margaret's affections drove away her partners when they were unable to meet the infinite nature of her expectations. Her fervor was simply too overwhelming. Anna Barker, Caroline Sturgis, Samuel Ward—each of these intense romances ended with their retreat away from Margaret. The harder she pressed, the further they drifted. In the most devastating heartbreak of her life, as Samuel Ward no long reciprocated her love, she learned he was engaged to her truest love—Anna. In a feat of magnanimity, she ultimately managed to give the two loves her blessing, recognizing that "feelings are the most perishable of our possessions" (Popova, p. 133).

WALDO & MARGARET

Ralph Waldo Emerson and Margaret Fuller had a unique relationship—a special intellectual bond that seemed to transcend all definition. However, Waldo was married, and his wife seldom cared for the amount of time he spent with Margaret. Margaret, searching for a definition to whatever their intense relationship was, begged Waldo to give it a name. But for his part, Waldo saw marriage as a prison and would never add the confines of another relationship to that punishment. In a series of letters, he asked Margaret to never ask him to define their uncommon relationship again.

Key Takeaway: Fuller's obsession with personal relationships was both her blessing and her tragedy.

Fuller wanted so badly to embrace "the All" and have it returned, that she became her own worst enemy. She believed she could work hard enough to make it happen, forgetting the most obvious fact that love is the one thing that must come without asking. From an intellectual standpoint, her understanding of gender as nonbinary—as no one being wholly masculine or wholly feminine—was groundbreaking and was the beginning of the feminist movement and the impetus for her "Conversations." But her highly intellectual approach to her own relationships was sure to doom them.

"However divided we may feel within ourselves, it is the sum total of our warring factions that makes us who we are—fragmentary but indivisible" (Popova, p. 154).

FULLER'S REVOLUTION OF THOUGHT

After an extended journey westward with her once-beau James Freeman Clarke and his sister Sarah in 1844, Fuller penned her first book, *Summer on the Lakes*. It challenged dogmatic religious beliefs and inspired to find a higher calling in democratic ideals and intellectualism. It was a massive success and piqued the interest of Horace Greeley, the founder of the *New York Tribune*.

Key Takeaway: Fuller becomes America's first female editor of a major paper.

Leaving Boston and her tortured relationship with Emerson behind, Fuller began working as a journalist and editor at the *New York Tribune*. She worked tirelessly to expose the inequalities and injustices she saw rife in America. She went into the coal mines and into prisons and mental institutions to highlight the horrendous conditions within. She wrote at length on art and beauty and truth. She wrote in support of abolition, women's rights, and against the death penalty (a very controversial stance at the time). She was both prolific and transcendent and received accolades from many prominent intellectuals of the period.

Key Takeaway: Fuller's *Woman in the Nineteenth Century* inspires many.

Based on an essay that was originally published in *The Dial*, Fuller expanded it into her seminal work: a Declaration of Independence for American women as well as a scathing criticism of the systemic inequalities and their vast disconnect from the principals of American democracy. Forty-three years later, Walt Whitman extolled the virtues of her once-radical ideas on equality.

Fuller also inspired Julia Ward Howe, who would go on to write "The Battle Hymn of the Republic" and a collection of provocative poetry titled *Passion Flowers*, among other things. Howe was trapped in a loveless, abusive marriage and surely found solace and courage in the words of Fuller, as well as in her friend Maria Mitchell. Both Mitchell and Howe, along with countless others, were inspired to action by Fuller's work.

WOMEN & EDUCATION

Fuller's book lit up a firestorm of change in America, demanding women freedom of thought, freedom of education, freedom to own property, and freedom to choose when and if they marry. Maria Mitchell was at the forefront of that change.

Key Takeaway: Maria Mitchell changes the face of female science education.

With a $3,000 gift that was essentially crowdfunded through the press, Mitchell opened an observatory on Nantucket welcoming both boys and girls. Twenty years after *Woman*, Mitchell would become the first female professor of astronomy at Vassar College. In her twenty-three years at the school, Vassar graduated more students in astronomy and higher math than Harvard (Popova, p. 176).

Key Takeaway: Fuller suffers another heartbreak and retreats to Europe.

In what was perhaps the first unambiguously romantic relationship of her life, Margaret Fuller fell in love with a man named James Nathan. Nathan, however, was sleeping with an English maiden who also secretly lived in his house. In the end, he was only using Fuller for her editorial connections at the *Tribune* and eventually left for London with his maiden, leaving Fuller devastated.

Key Takeaway: Fuller meets George Sand and Adam Mickiewicz.

George Sand—an androgynous woman known for her male attire and relationships with both men and women—and Fuller were mutual fans of one another's. She left a strong impression of admiration on Fuller. However, it was Mickiewicz who was truly transformative for Fuller. He was a Polish poet—widely regarded as Poland's greatest poet in history—and he spoke with a candor she had never before seen. He challenged her notions of sensual love, of virginity, of happiness, and propriety.

MARAGRET'S LOVE

In 1847, after many years of solitude and heartbreak, Margaret finally found love in an unintellectual Italian man named Ossoli. Ossoli barely spoke English and Margaret hardly any Italian, but somehow their connection was stronger than any Margaret had felt before. Most likely because it was so different, and wasn't based at all on her intellect.

Key Takeaway: Margaret embraces simple love.

Ossoli didn't have her intellect, but he was constant in his loving, soothing, and serving. He asked for nothing, but simply enjoyed being with Margaret. Though she left him for a time, she was drawn back to him after another intellectual heartbreak with Thomas Hicks. Though Ossoli did ask for her hand in marriage, she refused, as she saw it a social construct and a prison for women.

Key Takeaway: Margaret is pregnant in Italy.

Fuller had taken Mickiewicz's advice that life could not be lived fully without experiencing love fully—which meant to explore sexuality and sensuality. Though Fuller was unwilling to marry Ossoli, they embarked on a secret romantic relationship that led to her getting pregnant. With her frail constitution, she was sure she would die in childbirth. Though abortion was legal in America at the time, it was forbidden in Rome. Margaret's letters home from this tumultuous time alluded only mysteriously to her condition and her inability to travel. Eventually, she took his married name, and started signing her letters Margaret Fuller Ossoli, though no marriage certificate was ever found.

LIFE IN ROME

Margaret wasn't just living in Rome; she was inspired and uplifted by the spirit of the revolution there. She believed that America had fallen into a state of gluttony and self-absorption and that the Risorgimento was a cause worthy of her dedication. She survived childbirth and devoted much of her time to writing the story and success of the Italian revolution in 1861 while still working as a foreign correspondent for the *New York Tribune*.

Key Takeaway: Fuller redefines her meaning of love in her exploration of her connection with Ossoli, and again in motherhood.

Despite her long history of intellectual romances, Fuller ruminates in letters her realization that matters of the heart and spirit are rather more important: "integrity, unaffected kindness, constancy of affection." She offers these almost as a defense of her relationship with the unlettered Ossoli. But with motherhood comes a new opening in her heart, a wholly new understanding of the boundless love she has for her son Angelo, and she finally shares her secret with her friends and family back home. Though wanting to return, her friends back home are worried for what people will think of her situation: unmarried with an uneducated man ten years her junior and a bastard child in tow. Emerson urges her to stay in Italy and finish her book on the revolution, but the letter never finds her.

Key Takeaway: Margaret returns to America.

Destitute with barely any money to feed their child and revolution rampaging through Rome, Margaret and Ossoli decide to return to America on a cargo ship with baby Angelo, despite whatever judgments may be passed on arrival. Though not a superstitious woman by any stretch of the imagination, Margaret is plagued by a "bad feeling" before the trip. She writes letters to her loved ones to be sent on a different ship in case they don't make the journey.

The captain of the ship almost immediately succumbs to small pox, and Nino (their nickname for Angelo) is stricken as well, despite being inoculated in Rome. Somehow, luckily, the baby recovers from the smallpox, and we are left with news that their ship, the *Elizabeth* has reached the harbor in New York.

ILLNESS

In the autumn of 1850, just as Margaret and family were undertaking their journey to America, Charles Darwin was struck with tragedy. He and his wife's second daughter, Annie—his favorite—fell mysteriously ill.

Key Takeaway: Medicine of the time was rudimentary at best and barbaric at worst.

Though Darwin was a scientist through and through, and was extremely skeptical of many of the "alternative" practices of the day, he was willing to try anything to save his daughter. Traditional treatments for illness included arsenic, mercury, and lead as well as bloodletting and blistering to let the ailing humors seep out—a relic of ancient Greek medicine. Alternative therapies focused on hydrotherapy, clairvoyance, and homeopathy. Darwin succumbed to hydrotherapy for his own anxiety and vomiting (likely a mental, not physical condition) and found great success, but his daughter Annie would not be so lucky.

Key Takeaway: Migraines represented a connection between the physical and the emotional.

Sophia Peabody, sister of Elizabeth Peabody (at whose home Fuller's "Conversations" were held) and wife of Nathaniel Hawthorne, spent her life battling a condition that had yet to be diagnosed as migraines. Treatments often included opium, calomel (mercury) and cold water therapy.

Though the condition of ocular migraines was yet to be discovered, John Herschel (uncle of Caroline Herschel, the role model of one Maria Mitchell) noted their distinct geometrical nature in the field of vision while suggesting their connection to the subconscious. It would be another hundred years before Oliver Sacks released his groundbreaking work, *Migraine*.

CAMERA OBSCURA

The chapter opens with a brief history of the discovery of photography, from the camera obscura, a light-box used to project images for tracing dating back before Leonardo DaVinci, to the chemical process by which those images were made permanent. Though many ambitious minds were working to perfect the process, Tom Wedgwood was the first to use silver nitrate to create impressions. Unfortunately for him, the impressions made would disappear the longer they were exposed to light, and he died before he could perfect it. Henry Fox Talbot was the next to come close, but Louis Daguerre, on the other side of the Atlantic would beat him to it. Talbot, a student of Sir John's Herschel's, informed him of the Frenchman's eponymous invention—the daguerreotype. Though Talbot had his own process, the *calotype*, daguerreotypes had already taken hold in America. Yet it was Herschel who coined the word photograph in 1839.

Key Takeaway: The photography of stars changed the way we see the universe.

Early photographs were mostly of statues, which lent themselves to the long exposure times necessary and the neoclassical tastes of the day. Not long after its invention, however, cameras were paired with increasingly powerful telescopes to create astrophotography. The Harvard College Observatory began to amass their collection of glass plate images, employing a team of women (because they turned out to be better calculators than the men) to analyze and annotate the glass plates, making calculations that would become the basis for many future discoveries.

Key Takeaway: The more accessible a medium becomes, the more careless we become about what we put into it.

This was as true when pre-Victorian letters, expensive to post and time-consuming to receive, gave way to the express penny post as it was when film cameras gave way to smartphone cameras. The more we use it, the easier it is, the more banality it will contain—the less value we will place on the contents of the medium. We can now take a picture of anything in an instant and send it to anyone in the world, and that medium has become filled with snippets of our day-to-days rather than cherished, thoughtful moments.

HARRIET HOSMER

Harriet Hosmer, born in 1830 to a well-off physician, was to become the first successful female sculptor in America. Her childhood, after the loss of her mother and siblings to tuberculosis, was dictated to be filled with endless, vigorous outdoor activity as was prescribed by her father. At twenty-two, she received a medical degree (one of the first women in the country to do so) in order to better understand anatomy for her sculpture.

Key Takeaway: Hosmer's life was punctuated by love and loss.

Harriet saw the world for what it was: a mess of beauty and impermanence, joy and pain. As a lesbian (though the writer notes this term wouldn't be common for another hundred years) she fell in love with her best friend, who would then marry a man, breaking Hosmer's heart. Her first successful sculpture, *Hesper,* is thought to be a sort of tribute to the love she could never have.

Key Takeaway: Rome offered a solace both for artists and for queer culture in the nineteenth century.

Hatty, as she was known to friends, was known to dress in men's clothing and often kept the company of women. Charlotte Cushman and journalist Matilda Hays were the closest to what you could consider an "out lesbian couple" in those days. After sparking an immediate and intense connection with Cushman, and believing Rome was the only place she could truly develop her art, Hatty joined them both in Italy, along with her father, and took up an apprenticeship with famed English sculptor, John Gibson.

Hosmer's work excelled under her apprenticeship and in Rome's queer expat culture, addressing such modern feminist issues as victim-blaming in rape through the use of classical Greek mythology.

LIFE, LOVE & LOSS

During her time in Europe, Hatty grew into a new woman, barely recognizable to even herself as she explored her art and her sexuality. She became close friends with Robert and Elizabeth Barrett Browning, the couple becoming like parents to her. Hosmer also found a lover and a muse, a wealthy Scottish widow with whom she would spend the rest of her life, and the only living woman she would ever sculpt. Lady Louise Ashburton would refer to Hatty as "sposa" and Hatty to herself as Louisa's "hubby" or "wedded wife" (Popova, p. 298).

Key Takeaway: Hosmer creates two great masterpieces in her early twenties.

Zenobia in Chains and *Beatrice Censi* would solidify Hosmer as the preeminent female sculptor of her day. Beatrice was a 16th century Roman woman who was brutally raped by her father, brought his crimes to the authorities who did nothing, and was then executed for his murder when she took justice into her own hands. Zenobia was a third-century Persian queen who was highly intellectual and conquered much of the East Roman Empire until she was captured and exiled to Rome. Hosmer's statue depicted Zenobia in chains, but still proud and defiant. It became a symbol both of women's rights as well as the fight against slavery, currently raging in America.

Key Takeaway: Hosmer seeks immortality, but finds failure.

Hosmer's wildly successful career was destined to end with loss. After Lincoln's assassination, the neoclassical style of her work fell out of fashion and she was forced to reinvent herself. She turned to the sciences, aiming to create a marble-like material that was easier and cheaper to work with. She succeeded in that, but then her attention strangely shifted to creating a perpetual motion machine. Many, if not all great minds are interdisciplinary, but the author notes the particular poignancy of a woman who experienced so much loss in life—her father, mother, siblings, spouse—trying to find a way to manufacture impossible permanence in a field she knew almost nothing about.

EMILY DICKINSON

Far from the first mention of the famed Massachusetts poet in the book, the seventeenth chapter is the first completely devoted to her. Snippets of her verse appear in chapter after chapter, but this is the first glimpse into her private life afforded to the reader.

Key Takeaway: Dickinson struggled with forbidden romantic love.

The majority of the first chapter on Dickinson is dedicated to exploring the relationship between Emily and her best friend and life-long love, Susan Gilbert. Gilbert and Dickinson met in Amherst, Massachusetts in 1850 and quickly commenced an "intense, intimate correspondence that would evolve and permute but would last a lifetime" (Popova, p. 308). The chapter is rich with excerpts from Emily's letters to Susan, showing an ever-growing love from one, perhaps of friendship, to one undoubtedly overcome with passion and desire. As a testament to Emily's skewed sense of gender she often referred to herself as a man, using "bearded" pronouns or changing the genders in her poems written for Susan that they might conform to the accepted romantic gender roles of the time.

Later in life, Emily would engage in a more traditional courtship with Judge Otis Lord, and contemplated marriage, though he would die before the two of them had the chance.

Key Takeaway: Emily's life and work were defined by loneliness and heartache.

As we have seen with so many non-traditional female relationships in the nineteenth century, Emily's ardor was returned with increased distance from Susan. Whether or not Susan felt the same way but knew it was inappropriate, or genuinely felt only platonic love for Emily remains to be seen. But Susan eventually married Emily's brother Austin, with whom she was also very close. Emily's fear of death, of abandonment, of losing those she loved was an ever-common theme throughout her work, though which "terrors" she refers to in her work remains rife with speculation.

Key Takeaway: Much of Dickinson's life remains a mystery.

Even after her brother's marriage to Susan, Emily and her love remained in steadfast contact, living just across the way from one another, though often Emily would still post letters to her rather than hand-delivering. By the late 1860s, Emily was almost completely reclusive. She began dressing in all white and refused to see anyone, more often than not receiving guests through a closed door. Much of what little we know of her relationships is based solely on the letters she wrote. The replies she received and collected, she instructed her sister to burn upon her death. The intended recipient of Dickinson's "Master Letters"—a set of letters to an unknown correspondent—remains a matter of wild speculation. Popova suggests that rather than a male suitor, the letters are written to a figment of her imagination, or an idol such as Shakespeare, which was a common practice in the day.

Key Takeaway: The great mystery of Dickinson's "terror."

In 1861, Dickinson writes a letter to the publisher Higginson who would become her close confidant, editor, and champion for the rest of her life. It contains a verse which has been the subject of much scrutiny in the 150 years since her death.

> I had a terror—since September—I could tell to none, and so I sing, as the Boy does by the Burying Ground—because I am afraid.

Whether the terror was her heartbreak with Susan, yet another devastating heartbreak with a woman named Kate, the first onset of her supposed epilepsy (another scholarly speculation based on her poetry and reclusiveness), the beginning of the Civil War, or some combination of events, no one knows.

Key Takeaway: Dickinson's genius was greatly overlooked during her lifetime.

In fact, just eleven of her more than 1,700 poems were published during her lifetime. The first volume wouldn't be released until four years after her death, and even then was rejected for being too eccentric, unconventional, and avantgarde before finding success. Her best friend Susan, her confidante and editor Higginson—who was also a publisher but didn't find her work commercially viable—and a small handful of friends were the only ones who saw her genius. When she did try to publish, she was met with rejection or edits too massive for her to accept. In addition, Dickinson struggled with the very idea of fame, wanting to keep her poetry private lest it be ruined—perhaps preferring to be a ghost of a woman locked in a room.

Key Takeaway: Austin Dickinson's paramour becomes Emily's greatest champion.

Susan and Austin Dickinson may have loved one another in one sense of the word at one point in time, but their marriage was both loveless and sexless. It wasn't until Austin met Mabel Loomis Todd, the wife of an astronomer at Amherst College, that he experienced the boundless, all-encompassing nature of true love and infatuation. He and Mabel would go on to have an illicit affair under the Dickinson family roof, feasibly unbeknownst to reclusive Emily. Susan, however, was painfully aware of their tryst and would hate Mabel for the rest of her life. Ironically, considering many of Emily's poems were love poems to the wife of Mabel's love, Mable would end up becoming one of Emily's biggest champions, transcribing hundreds upon hundreds of her poems after her death and playing a key part in their eventual publication. Were it not for Mable, Susan, and Higginson—who all saw Emily's work for the genius that it was—her oeuvre may never have seen the light of day.

PALE BLUE DOT

Jumping ninety-one years ahead of Dickinson's death, we are taken to the launching of the Voyager spaceships in 1977. Humanity placed on these ships a "golden record" meant to be a message to any alien species who may encounter the ships in the universe. The record contained greetings in fifty-four languages, music from Beethoven, and the sounds of a human heart beating, among many other things. In

1990, as Voyager 1 was about to leave the solar system—the first spacecraft ever to do so—Carl Sagan asked NASA to turn the probe around to take a photo of Earth from four billion miles away. That photo, entitled "Pale Blue Dot" would show the planet as an almost imperceptible smudge against the vast blackness of the universe. Sagan would go on to opine on our place in the universe in a speech at Cornell University in 1994:

"The Earth is a very small stage in a vast cosmic arena. Think of the rivers of blood spilled by all those generals and emperors so that in glory and in triumph they could become the momentary masters of a fraction of a dot. Think of the endless cruelties visited by the inhabitants of one corner of the dot on scarcely distinguishable inhabitants of some other corner of the dot. How frequent their misunderstandings, how eager they are to kill one another, how fervent their hatreds. Our posturings, our imagined self-importance, the delusion that we have some privileged position in the universe, are challenged by this point of pale light" (Sagan, Carl speech at Cornell University, October 13, 1994).

RACHEL CARSON

From a very young age, Rachel Carson knew she was meant to be a writer. Her first story was published in 1918 at the age of eleven. In 1936, she received her first paycheck for a piece of writing. In 1949 she became chief editor of publications for the U.S. Fish and Wildlife Service. In 1952, at the age of forty-five, she won the National Book Award and the John Burroughs Medal for *The Sea Around Us* and was posthumously awarded the nation's highest honor: the Presidential Medal of Freedom. Carson's family was extremely poor, and she found success only through a long life of hard work and sacrifice.

Key Takeaway: Carson marries literature and science as no one before her.

While studying at Pennsylvania College for Women, Carson was introduced to the study of biology and switched her major from literature. However, what she was truly after was a marriage of the two disciplines, realizing that no understanding of poetry could be complete without a knowledge of science, and no science writing could truly capture the intensely personal and human nature of our understanding of the earth. She took a particular interest in marine biology and the mystery of life beneath the world's oceans.

After college, her first job was with the U.S. Bureau of Fisheries, where she was asked to translate field report data into brochures. Rather than a government document, she created a vivid narrative of a journey along the ocean floor. Deemed unfit by her boss for its government purpose, she instead submitted it, and it was published in the *Atlantic Monthly* in 1937. It would become the basis for her first book, *Under the Sea-Wind*.

Key Takeaway: Carson's second book finds commercial success.

Though *Under the Sea-Wind* met early critical success, its publication just before the bombing of Pearl Harbor meant it was lost in the tumult of World War II. Her second book, *The Sea Around Us*, was heralded by laymen, literati, and science minds alike for its uncanny delivery of lofty, poetry-like prose without sacrificing any of its scientific merit or widespread accessibility. Of course, in her success, Carson was still met with the sexist criticism of the day, many men refusing to admit a woman could equal a man in intelligence, and others still insisting to address her as sir.

Key Takeaway: Carson retreats to Maine and finds companionship.

Her wild success meant that Carson was finally financial stable after a life of hardship. She quit her job at the U.S. Fish and Wildlife Service and bought a home on the coast of Maine to focus on her next book, *The Edge of the Sea*. It was there she met a local woman, Dorothy Freeman. Freeman was married, but she and Carson embarked on an intensely intimate relationship, writing one another frequently, stealing time when they could, and there is rich speculation that she and Carson engaged in a physical relationship as well, albeit rarely.

Key Takeaway: Rachel and Dorothy shared a unique love.

Popova shares numerous excerpts of letters between the two women who loved each other so dearly, and who shared a unique and private understanding of one another. Though Freeman was beyond happy in her marriage, what she shared with Carson was something wholly different. At one point, Dorothy even shared some of their private correspondence with her husband, who, instead of being angry, was happy at the depth of love and appreciation between the two women. Both Popova and Freemen express the belief that love is not a zero-sum equation, with the love of one stealing from the love of another; the more we love and are loved, the more love we have to give.

Key Takeaway: Carson's work shifts towards conservation.

After the wild success of her third book, *The Edge of the Sea*—yet another poetic introspection into the marriage of nature, humanity, philosophy, and science—Carson began to focus on the "darker truths of humanity's relationship with nature" (Popova, p. 464). The political climate of the time saw Eisenhower elected and the stripping of legal protections that natural resources may be used to further the interests of big business. A 1953 article she wrote in *The Washington Post* calling for the preservation of these protections seems incredibly prescient today as climate change denial runs rampant and the Trump administration strips the same agencies of their power, replacing their leaders with political pawns.

NUCLEAR FISSION

The twenty-sixth chapter presents an interlude on the accidental discovery of nuclear fission by German scientists Lise Meitner and Otto Hahn along with Otto Frisch and Neils Bohr. When they saw that hitting the nucleus of a uranium atom with a single neutron changed the atomic number of the atom from 92 to 88 (transforming it into radium), they assumed the results were a mistake. When Meitner and Frisch first released their paper coining the term nuclear fission in 1938, neither of them could have fathomed the destruction it precipitated.

Key Takeaway: The creation of the atomic bomb represented man's ultimate destruction of nature and himself.

Popova points out the parallels between Carson's opinions on the widespread use of DDT and Lise Meitner's opinions on the "ghastly malevolence" of the creation of the atom bomb. Both creations, in their eyes, took the brilliance of groundbreaking scientific discovery and bastardized it into a way to kill the very planet that scientists were meant to exalt. In the acceptance speech for her National Book Award, Carson opined on man's inability to turn the telescope back on himself, so long was he preoccupied with turning it towards the heavens:

"Perhaps if we reversed the telescope and looked at man down these long vistas, we should find less time and inclination to plan for our own destruction" (Carson, p. 481).

RACHEL CARSON'S LEGACY

Key Takeaway: Carson takes up the fight against DDT.

Carson had been following the deleterious and understudied consequences of DDT for more than a decade at this point, though it seemed the research was reaching a fever pitch. People, fish, birds, and insects were dying all across the country, and the government refused to step in and do anything about it, going so far as to spray the poison randomly across private lands and crops. Despite Carson's own battle with breast cancer that would metastasize to her lymph nodes, she worked tirelessly to finish her most controversial and groundbreaking book, *Silent Spring*. Carson's research for the book was exhaustive, conclusive, and undeniable. She wanted it to be an irrefutable call to the horrors of unfettered modern science against nature and the environment.

Key Takeaway: *Silent Spring* is released to praise, skepticism, and denial.

Much like Darwin fighting against the Church with the release of *Origin of the Species*, so was the response to *Silent Spring* by a country whose policy was being dominated and paid for by the pesticide industry. While the public was outraged and demanded action, those in power insisted the benefits of pesticides outweighed the costs and dismissed Carson's book as causing "unnecessary hysteria"—a favorite word used to silence and discredit women throughout history.

The attacks against the book were far more than soundbites. The pesticide industry was threatening lawsuits for libel, even the Department of Agriculture—a longtime friend of the industry—was attempting to undermine her credibility by combing through old articles of hers. The most absurd charge to spring from their attack was that Carson was a Communist. Though most publications reviewed the book favorably, several notable ones, including *Time* and *The Economist*, sided with the pesticide industry presumably due to advertising dollars coming from chemical companies like Dow, DuPont, and Velsicol. The reviewer in *Time* used another famous anti-feminist sentiment, describing the book as "an emotional and inaccurate outburst" (Popova, p. 496).

Key Takeaway: It takes great courage to be the face of dissent.

From Kepler to Galileo to Descartes to Darwin, many have dared to speak against the status quo and suggest an alternate possibility for the way things are. Most of those who dare are met with, at best, derision, and at worse, physical torture. Galileo ultimately recanted his belief in the heliocentric model, and Kepler was barred from the Church. Descartes, upon seeing Galileo's fate, abandoned the publication of any of his philosophy of which the Church would disapprove.

Key Takeaway: Rachel Carson is vindicated.

After being attacked by the government, by the agriculture industry, the food industry, and the pesticide industry, Carson agreed to do an interview on *Silent Spring* for *CBS Reports*. When the show finally aired in 1963, featuring Carson along with heads of petrochemical companies and top government officials, the American people saw Carson as the clear winner. Robert H. White-Stevens, a commercial chemist and one of her most vocal opponents, came off as a desperately pushing capitalist propaganda, while the government officials came off as bumbling and equivocating. The book and the program led to John F. Kennedy creating a Science Advisory Committee to investigate the harmful effects of pesticides and eventually to the creation of the Environmental Protection Agency and the banning of DDT—though both of the latter would happen after Carson's death.

Key Takeaway: Carson's last year is success and sorrow.

Carson gave her testimony to the congressional committee on pesticides in the last year before her death. The cancer had ravaged her body and she spent one remaining summer enjoying the simple beauties of nature with the love of her life in Southport, Maine. In that year, though she was confined to a wheelchair and in constant agony, she refused to let the public know she was ill. She received the highest medal from the National Audubon Society, the American Geographical Society medal, and was admitted to the American Academy of Arts and Letters, the last an honor reserved for only fifty artists and cementing her merit not just as a science writer, but as a literary genius.

When she finally died of a heart attack in April, 1964, she wished to be cremated with her ashes spread at Southport and a passage about the transience of Monarch butterflies—Dorothy's favorite passage—to be read at the service. Instead, her long-estranged brother who disapproved of her lifestyle ransacked her house, destroyed her incendiary writings, and arranged a highly public funeral and burial that, by all accounts of those who knew her, was exactly the opposite of what she wanted. While the public mourned publicly, those who loved her convinced her brother to allow part of her to be spread to the sea and held their own private ceremony according to Rachel's wishes.

INTO THE SEA

The final chapter of the book takes us back to Margaret Fuller with her perhaps-husband Ossoli and their baby, Nino. The boat is almost to the New York harbor. Nino survived the smallpox. They had made it after all.

But what they thought was the harbor was only Fire Island. After the captain had died of smallpox, an inexperienced sailor had taken them off course. A storm breaks and the boat is suddenly being swallowed into the sea; a sailor takes baby Nino trying to save him; Margaret and Ossoli refuse to leave the boat unless together. No one from the shore bothers to row the lifeboat out three miles to rescue the passengers. The sailor, the baby, Margaret, and Ossoli would all drown that night. Along with their bodies, Fuller's manuscript on the Italian Revolution was lost to the sea forever.

KEY THEMES

Identity

As a young girl, Margaret Fuller asked herself, "How is it that I seem to be this Margaret Fuller? What does it mean?" And perhaps spent her life trying to answer that question. We are different people, yet we are always the same, a collection of all the people we ever were. We try to carve out a solid sense of self, but nothing is really the same from one decade to the next.

Not only are we different people throughout our lives, but we are different people during them too. Dickinson was a different person to her beloved Susan than to her sister Lavinia or to her brother Austin. We are each prisms of personalities.

"These are not costumes donned with artifice for different occasions—they are facets of a self, each illuminated when a particular beam hits at a particular angle" (Popova, p. 397).

Transformation

Popova presents a story of Einstein seeing a construction worker fall from a height. Luckily, he is unharmed, but he rushes over to ask him if he felt the pull of gravity as he sped toward the earth. He did not. This lack of understanding of the forces working on us both informed Einstein's theory of relativity as well as parallels our understanding of our own transformations. It is impossible for us to see how much different we are when we are in the midst of such upheaval. Popova's narrative follows the transformations of so many people, how they were affected, by whom, and how they saw themselves through their own letters and correspondences. Only in rare moments are we able to see with clear vision our own transformations.

Feminism & Sexuality

No discussion of this book would be complete without mentioning the two currents that quietly carry the narrative from one woman to the next: feminism and sexuality. With each female achievement mentioned, Popova meticulously describes the hurdles they had to overcome, the men who scoffed at the them, and the doors that were closed to them. With each love letter from one woman to another, Popova investigates the nature of queer sexuality in a time when such a thing didn't exist in the lexicon of society.

Impermanence & Ephemerality

Popova's work ranges from universal to infinitesimal, comparing both the distance of the galaxies and the size of the atom. In all of this, humanity is yet another nothing. As Carson once looked out to the sea, she noted the coast that was once a plain of sand and would once again return to sand in the eons of earth's past and future. Even the things we think are the most permanent—the mountains, the Sun, the stars—each of them will become something else in their own time. With the invention of the photograph, which perhaps led us to believe we were finding some slice of immortality, it instead shows that while the photograph may outlast us, our bodies still turn to dust.

"There are no overtones of sentimentality in entropy's unceasing serenade to the cosmos" (Popova, p. 262).

Interconnection

One aspect of the book this summary is unable to fully convey is the sheer volume of interconnectedness of the stories Popova retells. Each chapter is rich with how one great mind knew another, how they crossed paths at a certain observatory or music hall; what one brilliant writer was working on in Rome while another was publishing their seminal work in Boston. But of course, beyond the interconnectedness of genius throughout the story, is the interconnectedness of everything else—indeed of everything in existence.

Surely this inextricability of science, poetry, ecology, humanity, power, and life is the overarching theme of the book—the thesis on which Popova endeavored to write such a history-spanning work. With Mitchell's love for poetry, Emerson's love for astronomy, with Whitman's odes to nature, and with Carson's unprecedented ability to make accessible the very human spirit that lies at the center of scientific inquiry, and the undeniable beauty in all of those things—Popova expertly presents a case that to silo these disciplines is to strip them of their very essence. The intersection of astronomy, poetry, and the transcendentalist philosophy (and their reverence for the spiritual in nature) undeniably fomented the environmental movement. The environmental movement, and Carson's work in particular, showed us beyond a shadow of a doubt that no action can be taken in a vacuum—that everything man attempts to do in this world will have farther-reaching effects than any one of us could imagine. Without striving to see our own humanity in nature—and nature in our own humanity—we are doomed to destruction.

EDITORIAL REVIEW

Maria Popova's *Figuring* is a transcendent work of astronomy, history, biography, chemistry, poetry, ecology, literature, philosophy, and wonder.

From Kepler in the sixteenth century to Carson in the twentieth, Popova's narrative attempts to seamlessly weave together the personal lives of a cast of characters who would indelibly change society with their work. Though thoroughly researched, and rich with excerpts, the book is far from academic. Meant to pay homage to the great women and men within its pages, it would be done a disservice were it not to be accoladed for its own poetic prose. Her words are moving and thoughtful, often indistinguishable from the grace and quality of the timeless literature she references.

Popova uses the brilliance and insight of many before her to limn the both vast and infinitesimal nature of the universe. Her writing calls to the reader to look beyond themselves, to find their higher nature and live in what Goethe would refer to as—and what Margaret Fuller would continuously come back to— "the All."

So much in the world matters so much to us—love, grief, loneliness—yet ultimately no one can truly matter in the grand scheme of the universe. That's not to discount the value of love and compassion, but rather to underscore it. If success and power and conquering lands don't matter on this pale blue dot, then love and compassion are the only things that do. Living beyond ourselves is the only way to escape the ephemeral nature of who we are.

If there is a criticism of the book to be made (and many reviewers have already made it), it is Popova's tendency to wander off course or indulge a tangent. Chapters on Richard Feynman, migraines, Carl Sagan's "Pale Blue Dot," and the history of nuclear fission don't fall as easily into the narrative as others, nor weave back into it, though their relevance isn't completely lost. While some readers may be off-put by the overwhelming web of seemingly insignificant connections from one moment to the next, others may find it a fascinating web in which to be caught.

From an academic standpoint, the book is a well-cited history of the natural progression from transcendentalism to environmentalism and a call to action to continue Carson's work; from a scientific standpoint, it is a celebration of the achievements of determined women in fields they were long excluded from; from a social-historical standpoint, it is an exposition on queer culture and feminism long glossed over in formal history books; from a philosophical standpoint, it is a rumination on the meaning of life, love, and the universe; from a literary standpoint, it is a moving, epistolary enquiry into the power of words on ourselves and others. In the end, no book summary can do justice to a work spanning space, time, society, discipline, and gender such as Popova has created.

TIMELINE OF EVENTS

1828 – Caroline Herschel is the first woman awarded the Gold Medal at the Royal Astronomical Society

1831 – Mary Somerville releases *The Mechanism of the Heavens*

1839 – Photography is born, the term coined by John Herschel

1839 – Margaret Fuller begins hosting her "Conversations" for women at Elizabeth Peabody's home in Boston, MA

1840 – Fuller and Emerson publish the first edition of *The Dial*

1844 – Margaret Fuller becomes the first female editor of a major newspaper, the *New York Tribune*

1845 – Margaret Fuller publishes her revolutionary book, *Woman in the Nineteenth Century*

1846 – Margaret Fuller moves to Europe

1847 – Maria Mitchell discovers her comet, "Miss Mitchell's Comet"

1847 – Florence Nightingale becomes head of a nursing staff during the Crimean War.

1848 – Maria Mitchell is the first woman elected fellow of the American Academy of Arts and Sciences

1850 – Emily Dickinson and Susan Gilbert begin their lifelong relationship

1850 – Herman Melville and Nathaniel Hawthorne first meet

1850 – Margaret Fuller Ossoli and her family return to New York

1856 – Elizabeth Barrett Browning publishes her epic novel/poem, *Aurora Leigh* that would go on to inspire Mitchell and Dickinson, among many others

1859 – Harriet Hosmer creates her masterpiece, *Zenobia in Chains*

1859 – Charles Darwin publishes *On the Origin of the Species*

1865 – Maria Mitchell becomes the first female professor of astronomy at Vassar College

1886 – Emily Dickinson dies of unknown causes

1890 – Emily Dickinson's first volume, *Poems*, is published posthumously

1920 – The 19th Amendment for women's suffrage passes

1952 – Rachel Carson wins the National Book Award for *The Sea Around Us*

BACKGROUND ON AUTHOR

Maria Popova is a Bulgarian-born writer, blogger, and literary and cultural critic currently living in Brooklyn, New York. She graduated from the American College of Sofia in Bulgaria in 2003 before attending the University of Pennsylvania and earning a degree in communications.

Popova is most notable for her blog, Brain Pickings, which covers a wide variety of cultural topics including history, current events, literature, and art. She has also written for *The Atlantic*, *Wired UK*, *Good Magazine*, *The Huffington Post*, and *Nieman Journalism Lab*.

In 2012, she was named one of the 51 most creative people in business by *Fast Company* magazine and was featured in *Forbes'* 30 under 30 in the same year.

Titles by Maria Popova

Figuring (2019)

A Velocity of Being: Letters to a Young Reader Co-edited with Claudia Bedrick.*(2018)*

****End of Book Summary****

*If you enjoyed this **ZIP Reads** publication, we encourage you to purchase a copy of the original book.*

We'd also love an honest review on Amazon.com!

Want **FREE** book summaries delivered weekly? Sign up for our email list and get notified of all our new releases, free promos, and $0.99 deals!

No spam, just books.

Sign up at **www.zipreads.co**

ZIPREADS